COS/CH

D0185779

Stuff
to know
when you start
school
SCHOOL

Editor Hélène Hilton
Design and Illustration Charlotte Bull
Editorial Assistance Violet Peto
Additional Design and Illustration Rachael Hare
Producer, Pre-Production Dragana Puvacic
Producer John Casey
Educational Consultant Penny Coltman
Jacket Designer Charlotte Bull
Jacket Coordinator Francesca Young
Managing Editor Penny Smith
Managing Art Editor Mabel Chan
Publisher Mary Ling
Art Director Jane Bull

First published in Great Britain in 2018 by
Dorling Kindersley Limited
80 Strand, London, WC2R 0RL

Copyright © 2018 Dorling Kindersley Limited
A Penguin Random House Company
10 9 8 7 6 5 4 3 2 1
001–307863–May/2018

All rights reserved.
No part of this publication may be reproduced, stored in or introduced into a retrieval system, or transmitted, in any form, or by any means (electronic, mechanical, photocopying, recording, or otherwise), without the prior written permission of the copyright owner.

A CIP catalogue record for this book is available from the British Library.
ISBN: 978-0-2413-1618-4

Printed and bound in China

A WORLD OF IDEAS:
SEE ALL THERE IS TO KNOW

www.dk.com

Contents

4 All about you!

6 Who's in your family?

8 How do you feel today?

10 Very important manners

12 Pants go first

14 What will you wear today?

16 Squeaky clean

18 Sparkly teeth

20 Toilet time

22 Your first sleepover

24 Your amazing body

26 Happy heart

28 Look at all this food!

30 You and the Universe

32 Look after our planet

34 Very important living things

36 Stay safe

38 Sing and sign

40 Sing and learn

42 How to be a really good friend

44 Look at what I can do!

46 Hello school!

48 Index

All about you!

From the colour of your eyes to the shape of your nose, you are one of a kind from the day you are born. And every day since then, you've become even more special.

No one in the whole world looks like you. We all have different faces and bodies, as well as different hair, eye, and skin colours.

You are completely unique, totally special, and perfectly you.

No matter how you look, you are perfect just as you are.

All the things that you like, from your favourite toys to the friends and family you love, also make you who you are.

The choices you make are also a part of you. Being kind and friendly are choices that you make every day. What will you choose today?

Your name is who you are!

Practise writing the letters in your name to learn how to spell it.

Here are some ways you can practise.

With a pen or pencil on paper

With pebbles

With playdough

In the air with your finger

With a stick in the sand

In a steamed-up mirror or window

Who's in your family?

Your family is made up of the people who look after you, make you feel safe, and love you no matter what.

New siblings

Is there a new baby in your family?

Congratulations!

Here are some things you can do together to be friends.

Cuddle the baby.

Play with the baby.

Read to the baby.

Talk to the baby.

Babies cry because they can't talk yet, but babies can understand words before they can speak. Chat to your baby to help them learn faster.

How do you feel today?

Emotions are important because they tell you how you feel. All your feelings are worth listening to.

Face game

Can you guess how the people around you are feeling today? **How can you tell?**

I'm all shy!

If you feel shy, sometimes words just don't want to come out. That's okay, you just need to take a deep breath. You will get more confident with some practise.

What are tears?

Tears are drops of salty water that come from a pouch near the eye. People cry when they are sad or hurt, but also if they are happy and laughing. Weird!

Very important manners

Being **polite** shows others that you **care** about their feelings. Your best manners make people **smile**!

If you need to interrupt someone or get their attention, say "**excuse me**".
Excuse me!
This is really important.
Bye!
See you later!
Don't forget to say "**goodbye**" when you leave.
I am really, really
sorry
I hurt your feelings.
Apologising shows that you know you were wrong and won't do it again.
Nervous giggles
Lots of children giggle when they are told off because they feel embarrassed. If this happens to you, try to stay calm and listen so that you can learn.

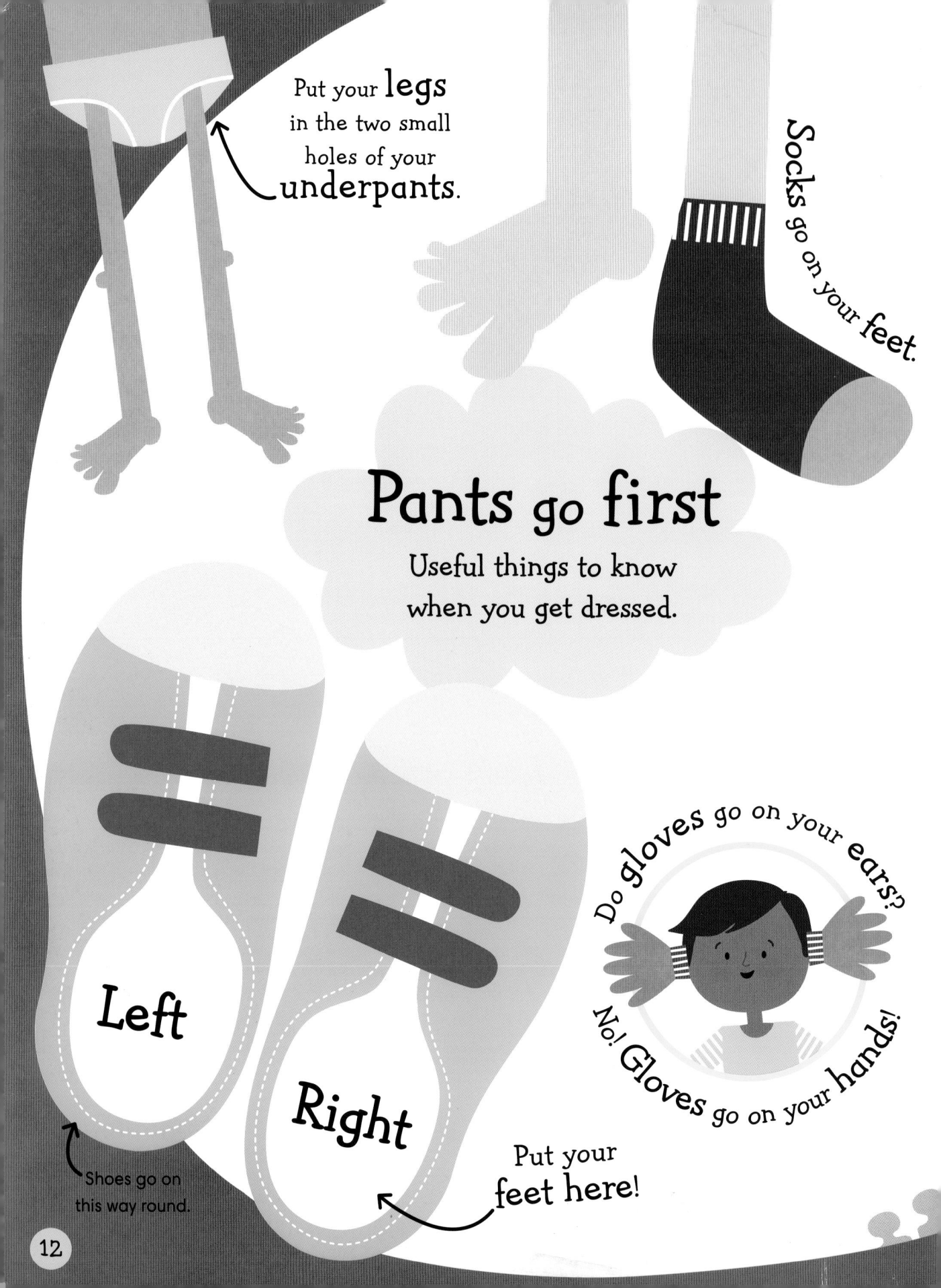
Put your legs in the two small holes of your underpants.
Socks go on your feet.
Pants go first
Useful things to know when you get dressed.
Left
Right
Do gloves go on your ears?
No! Gloves go on your hands!
Shoes go on this way round.
Put your feet here!

Shoelaces can be tricky when you start off, so ask someone to show you how to do it. If you practise lots you'll be doing your own laces very soon!

Zip or buttons?

Most buttons are done up by putting the button through the **buttonhole.**

Zips are made up of little teeth that come together to close. Pull the zip up to bring the teeth together.

Check the label so you put your top the right way round. The label goes in the back.

Try laying out your clothes on the floor before putting them on to make sure they're not inside out.

What will you wear today?

Pick the perfect clothes for you to wear today.

Spring

In **spring**, there are showers and rainbows. **Can you find a raincoat, welly boots, an umbrella, and a rain hat?**

Summer

In **summer**, the weather is sunny and hot. **Can you find a sunhat, sunglasses, shorts, a T-shirt, and sandals?**

Autumn

In **autumn**, the weather is cool and windy.

Can you find a jumper, a scarf, trousers, and shoes?

Winter

In **winter**, it's cold and it sometimes snows.

Can you find snow boots, a coat, a woolly hat, and gloves?

Squeaky clean
from head to toe

Here's a little guide to making sure you always feel (and smell) as fresh as a daisy.

But WHY do I have to be clean?

Apart from making sure you don't become all smelly and itchy, being clean helps to keep germs away.

Tissues ready!

Blow your nose by closing your mouth and blowing as hard as you can, out of your nostrils into a tissue.

Catch those germs!

Cover your mouth when you cough to stop germs spreading to other people. Then wash your hands.

Wash your hands!

Keep your hands germ-free with lots of soap and water, especially before eating.

Look after your nails

Your nails keep growing all the time. Have them clipped to keep them short and tidy.

Shower time

Take a shower or a bath to wash yourself with lots of soap. Make shower time more fun by singing as loudly as you can!

Brush your hair

Brush or comb your hair to keep it from getting all tangled.

Shampoo makes your hair shiny and clean. Keep your eyes closed!

Hello, teeth!
I'm a front tooth, an **incisor**. My sharp edge cuts food.
I'm a side tooth, a **canine**. I am pointy to tear food.
I'm a big back tooth, a **molar**. I mash food into tiny bits.
Sparkly teeth
Your teeth need you to look after them so they stay **healthy** and sparkling. Brush them **twice a day** for **two whole minutes**.
Dentists are special teeth doctors. They check and clean your teeth to make sure they are healthy.
Wobbly tooth
When you're ready for grown-up teeth, your milk teeth get all wobbly and fall out. That makes a space for your big teeth!

But WHY should I brush my teeth?

Brushing helps to protect your teeth against germs that make little holes (cavities) in your teeth.

Sugary things like fizzy drinks and sweets can also damage your teeth.

How to brush your teeth (and do a really, really good job)

1. Squeeze a little blob of toothpaste onto your toothbrush.
2. Move your brush up and down over your teeth.
3. Keep brushing for two minutes, making sure you brush the front, back, and underneath of your teeth.
4. Spit out the toothpaste and rinse your toothbrush.
5. All done! Your teeth are sparkly clean and minty fresh.

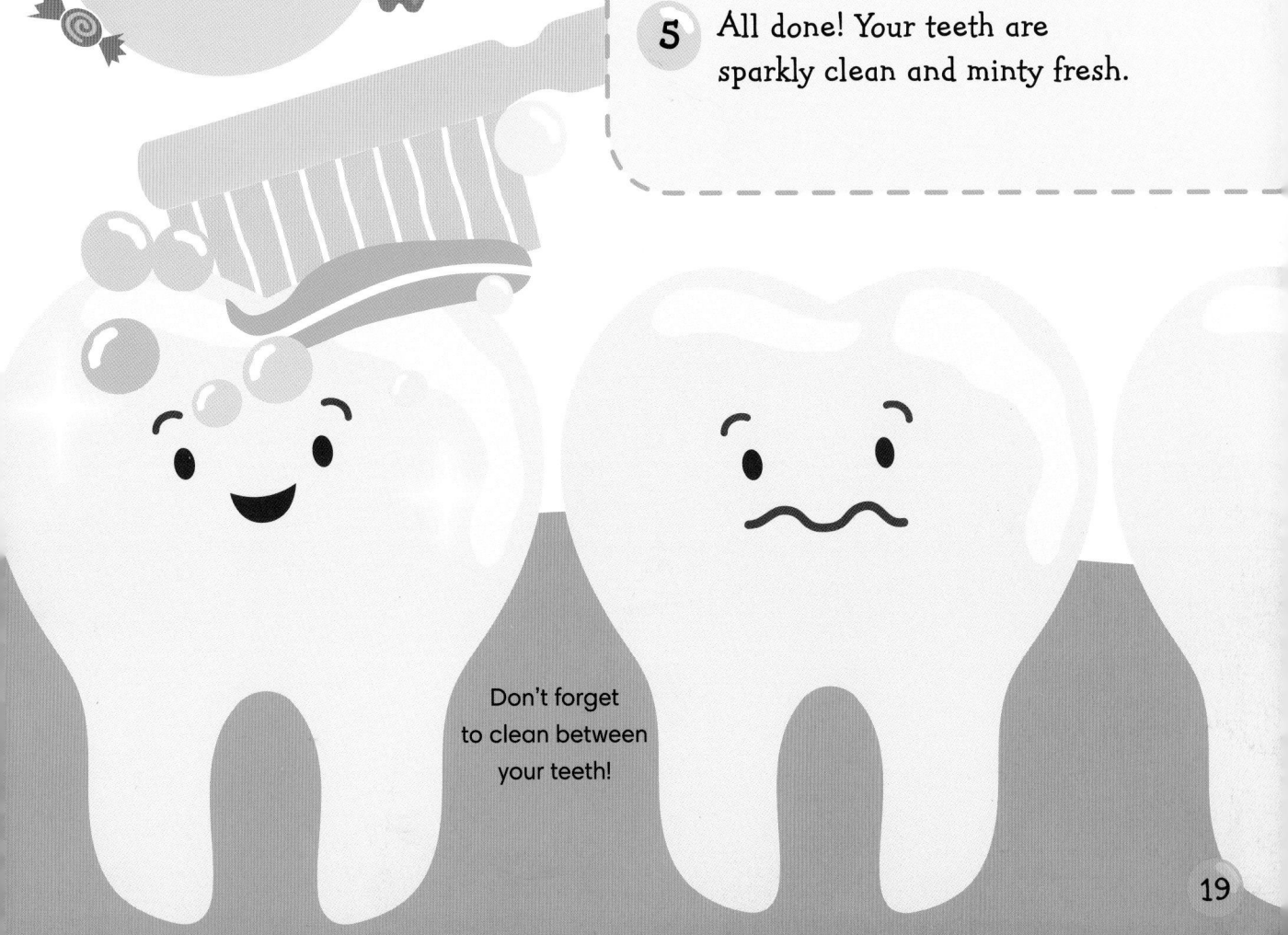

Don't forget to clean between your teeth!

Toilet time

If it's time to be out of nappies, it's time to learn what to do with a grown-up toilet.

If you need the toilet, don't wait until it's an emergency.

Toilets outside of houses, like at school or in restaurants, can be different to the toilets you have at home. If you feel unsure about them, check with a grown-up.

1. Sit on the toilet.
2. Do your business.
3. Wipe with toilet paper until you're all clean.
4. Flush!
5. Wash your hands.

Carefully, with soap and water. (EVERY TIME!)

Night-time accidents

If you have an accident while you sleep, it's not your fault. Lots of children wet the bed so don't be embarrassed. Bed wetting goes away all on its own after a while.

Your first sleepover

Sleepovers are so much fun! Whose house are you sleeping at tonight?

Don't forget your favourite cuddly toy.

Follow the wiggly line to get all ready for bed.

Say good night

Lights out!

Spooky dark

Not being able to see what's around you can be worrying. But if you can't have a night-light, remind yourself that you are safe in your bed.

Put your pyjamas on
Brush your teeth
Bedtime story
Go to the toilet
Sweet dreams
I love sleepovers at my grandparents' house. I always get a bedtime story.

Your amazing body

From the top of your head, to the tips of your toes, your body is perfect.

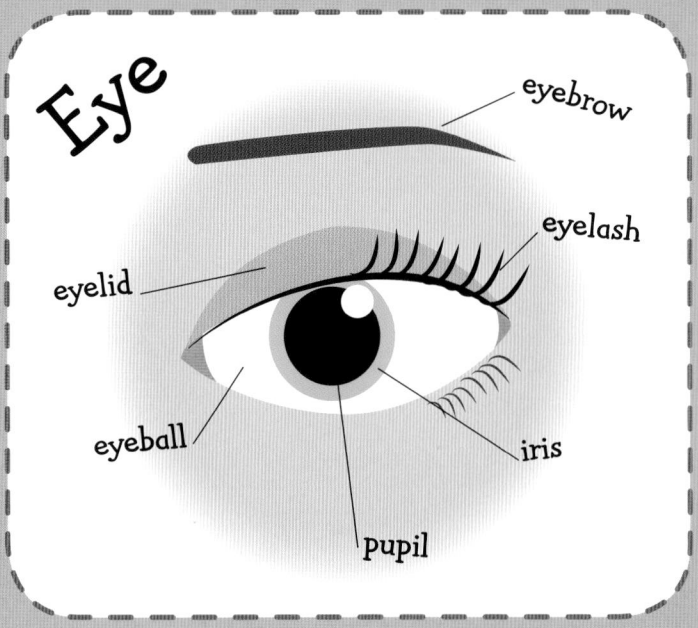

Head

Do you know what your **body parts** are called?

hair
eye
ear
nostril
nose
cheek
teeth
mouth
lips
chin
neck
shoulder
arm
elbow
wrist
palm
thumb
hand
finger

Body
chest
stomach
belly button
hip
leg
knee
foot
toe
Eat well
Your body needs you to eat different types of food to stay strong and healthy. Here are some things you should eat every day:
Lots of **fruit** and **vegetables.**
Some starchy food, like **bread** or **rice.**
Some protein, such as **meat**, **eggs**, or **beans**.
Some healthy oil, like **avocados** or **nuts**.
Move your body
You are meant to move, run, jump, dance, and use lots of energy. Your body needs to exercise to stay strong.
Some of your body parts, like your skeleton and your heart, are hidden away inside of you.

Happy heart

Feeling happy is one of the best things in the world!

What makes you happy?

being read to

cuddly toys

hugs

painting

Sleepy time

Your body and your mind need sleep to feel ready for a new day. Children need to sleep for around 10 or 11 hours every night.

Draw a picture of all the things that make you happy. Think about the people who make you smile and the things you love doing.

No one can be happy all the time. The best you can do is to keep trying to be happy as often as you can!

Look at all this food!

There is so much food to try and taste. Which of these are your favourites?

orange
strawberries
pineapple
olive oil
grapes
apple
watermelon
blackberries
kiwi
fish
honey
meat
milk
eggs
All the food that we eat either comes from a plant or an animal.

You and the Universe

Our planet Earth is just one tiny weeny little planet in the whole big wide Universe!

Look at the sky at night to see far away stars and planets. No one knows how big the Universe is. It might go on forever and ever.

Earth is the only planet we know of in the whole Universe that has living things (like you) on it.

Our Solar System

Earth is one of eight planets that spin around the Sun. Together they make up the Solar System.

Look after our planet

Our planet Earth looks after us by giving us food, water, and energy. But we also need to look after the Earth before it becomes too damaged.

You can help save our planet Earth.

Grow some of your own food or buy food that was grown close to home.
Turn switches off to save energy.
Make your garden friendly to little animals that might need to live there.
What can I do to help?
Plant a tree. Trees make the air cleaner.
Recycle your rubbish.
Walk or cycle rather than drive to save fuel.

Very important living things

There are so many different animals and plants in the world that we still haven't discovered all of them. Which of these do you already know?

Plants and animals are things that are alive.
duck
flower
crab
rabbit
leaves
snail
ants
tiger
elephant
tree
dragonfly
goldfish
horse
human
Living things need to be looked after. Animals can't talk, but they can feel pain so it's important to be nice to them.
frog

Stay safe

You are a very special person so learn to keep yourself safe and sound.

Never speak to **someone you don't know on the Internet or in real life** without checking with a grown-up first.

Your body belongs to you.
No one should ever ask or make you do anything with your body that you don't want to do.
Don't **keep secrets** that make you sad or worried.
If you see anything on a **computer, phone, or tablet** that upsets you, walk away and go and tell you a grown-up.
!
Don't play near railway lines.
What number should you call in an emergency?
1 2
4 5 6
7 8 9
0
Always talk to someone you trust if you are feeling sad or worried.
Here are some people you can talk to:
someone in your family you trust
a police officer
a doctor
a nurse
someone at nursery or school

Sing and sign

Here are some fun songs you can sing
and act out with your hands.

Itsy bitsy spider climbed up the waterspout.

Down came the rain and washed the spider out.

Out came the sun and dried up all the rain

And itsy bitsy spider climbed up the spout again.

Round and round the garden

Like a teddy bear.

One step, two step,

Tickle you under there.

This little piggy went to market.

This little piggy stayed at home.

This little piggy had roast beef.

This little piggy had none.

And this little piggy went...

"Wee, wee, wee," all the way home.

If you're happy and you know it, clap your hands.

If you're happy and you know it, clap your hands.

If you're happy and you know it,

and you really want to show it.

If you're happy and you know it,

clap your hands!

Sing and learn

Learn some super-useful things
as you sing your little heart out!

You can sing
the Alphabet Song
to the tune of Twinkle,
Twinkle, Little Star.

Alphabet Song

A B C D E F G

H I J K L M N O P

Q R S T U and V

W X Y and Z

Now I know my ABC,

Next time won't you
sing with me?

The Alphabet Song teaches
you the names of all the
letters. Do you know what
sound the letters make
when they are in words?

Fish and count to 10

1, 2, 3, 4, 5,

Once I caught a fish alive.

6, 7, 8, 9, 10

Then I let it go again.

Why did you let it go?

Because it bit my finger so.

Which finger did it bite?

This little finger on my right!

How to be a really good friend

Friends are so much fun! Here are some tips to make lots of new friends.

NO!
If you've upset someone, try to understand what you have done wrong, and say "sorry".
If someone is being mean to you or to someone else, say "NO!", tell them how they are making you feel, and let a grown-up know straight away.
Take turns so that you can each have a go. Be fair!
What's a bully?
Bullies pick on others. Often bullies are people who don't know how to make friends so they act mean to feel included. If someone is bullying, you should tell a grown-up, but you could also show the bully how to be kind and play nicely.

Look at what I can do!

Here is a whole bunch of **awesome** stuff you can try, too. **You can do it!**

- [ ] Ride a bike or scooter
- [ ] Swim with swimming aids
- [ ] Make an obstacle course
- [ ] Climb a tree (carefully)
- [ ] Build a nature den
- [ ] Make mud art
- [ ] Play catch
- [ ] Go on a colour hunt

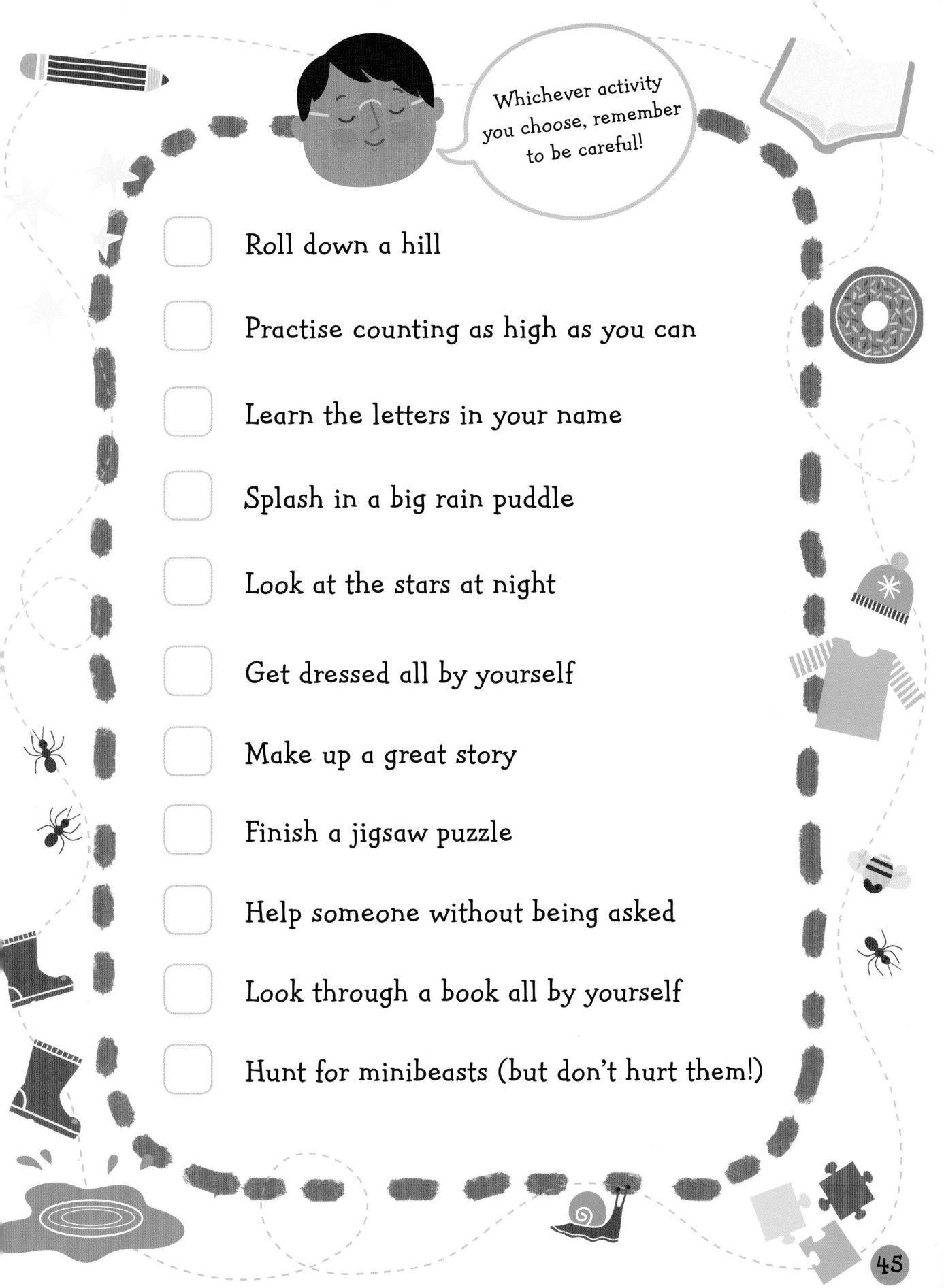

Whichever activity you choose, remember to be careful!

- [ ] Roll down a hill
- [ ] Practise counting as high as you can
- [ ] Learn the letters in your name
- [ ] Splash in a big rain puddle
- [ ] Look at the stars at night
- [ ] Get dressed all by yourself
- [ ] Make up a great story
- [ ] Finish a jigsaw puzzle
- [ ] Help someone without being asked
- [ ] Look through a book all by yourself
- [ ] Hunt for minibeasts (but don't hurt them!)

Hello, school!
SCHOOL
It's your first day of school! There are so many new things to say "hello" to.
Hello, playground
Hello, classroom

Hello,
friends
Hello,
coat peg
Hello,
head
teacher
Hello,
teacher
Hello,
toys
Say "see you later" to Mum and Dad. They'll be back after school.

Index

A
Accidents 21
Alphabet 40
Animals 29, 33, 34-35, 38-39

B
Baby 7
Bedtime 21, 22-23
Body 24-25, 26, 37
Bully 43

C
Clean 16-17, 18, 19
Clothes 13, 14-15
Counting 41, 45

E
Earth 30-31, 32-33
Emotions 8-9
Exercise 25

F
Family 5, 6-7, 27
Food 18, 25, 28-29, 33
Friends 5, 7, 27, 42-43, 47

G
Germs 16

H
Heart 25, 26

I
Internet 36

L
Left and right 12
Letters 5, 40, 45

M
Manners 10-11

P
Pets 27
Planet 30-31, 32-33
Plants 29, 34, 35
Playing 27, 42

R
Recycling 32-33

S
Safety 36-37
School 20, 46-47
Seasons 14-15
Shoelaces 13
Sleep 21, 22-23, 26
Song 38-39, 40-41
Stars 30, 45

T
Teeth 18-19, 23, 24
Toilet 20-21, 23

U
Universe 30-31

Acknowledgements

The publisher would like to thank the following for their kind permission to reproduce their photographs:

(Key: a-above; b-below/bottom; c-centre; f-far; l-left; r-right; t-top)

28 Dreamstime.com: Leszek Ogrodnik / Lehu (c, cr); Tracy Decourcy / Rimglow (c/Carrot); Pichest Boonpanchua / Khumthong (br). **29 Dreamstime.com:** Leszek Ogrodnik / Lehu (ca). Getty Images: Burazin / Photographer's Choice RF (cra). **34 123RF.com:** Eric Isselee / isselee (crb/Polar bear cub); Ievgen Kovalev / genjok (cb). **Dreamstime.com:** Irochka (cb/Sunflower); Isselee (crb). **Fotolia:** Eric Isselee (cl). **35 Dreamstime.com:** Liligraphie (cl); Natalya Aksenova (tc). **iStockphoto.com:** Taalvi (crb)

All other images © Dorling Kindersley
For further information see: www.dkimages.com